Table of Contents

Chapter 1: Welcome to Białystok 4
1.1 Introduction to Białystok 5
1.2 A Brief History of Białystok 7
1.3 Geographical Overview 8
1.4 Białystok's Climate and Best Times to Visit 9
Chapter 2: Getting to and Around Białystok 11
2.1 Transportation to Białystok 12
2.2 Public Transportation within the City 15
2.3 Renting a Car or Bicycle 16
2.4 Walking Tours and Exploring on Foot 17
Chapter 3: Top Attractions in Białystok 18
3.1 Branicki Palace and Gardens 19
3.2 Białystok Historical Museum 20
3.3 Podlasie Opera and Philharmonic 21
3.4 St. Roch's Basilica 22
3.5 Białystok Market Square and City Hall 23
3.6 Lubomirski Palace 24
3.7 Parks and Green Spaces 25
3.8 Day Trips and Nearby Attractions 26
Chapter 4: Art and Culture 27
4.1 Art Galleries and Museums 28
4.2 The Białystok Theater Scene 29
4.3 Annual Festivals and Events 30
4.4 The Jewish Heritage and Synagogues 32
Chapter 5: The Culinary Scene in Białystok 34
5.1 Traditional Polish Dishes to Try 35
5.2 Popular Local Restaurants 37
5.3 Local Markets and Specialty Foods 39
5.4 Breweries and Nightlife 40
5.5 Food and Cultural Events 42

Chapter 6: Outdoor Activities and Nature 43
6.1 Hiking and Nature Trails 44
6.2 Biking Routes and Rentals 46
6.3 Białowieża Forest Day Trips 47
6.4 Boat Trips and Water Sports 48
6.5 Family-Friendly Outdoor Spots 49
Chapter 7: Accommodations in Białystok 50
7.1 Hotels in Białystok 51
7.2 Budget-Friendly Hostels 52
7.3 Boutique Hotels and Unique Stays 53
7.4 Vacation Rentals and Apartments 54
7.5 Family-Friendly Accommodation Options 55
Chapter 8: Shopping in Białystok 56
8.1 Shopping Malls and Department Stores 57
8.2 Local Artisan Shops 58
8.3 Souvenirs and Gifts 59
8.4 Farmers Markets and Local Produce 60
Chapter 9: Białystok for Families and Kids 61
9.1 Kid-Friendly Attractions 62
9.2 Outdoor Parks and Playgrounds 63
9.3 Family-Friendly Dining 64
9.4 Educational Museums and Activities 65
Chapter 10: Practical Information and Traveler Tips 66
10.1 Safety and Emergency Contacts 67
10.2 Health and Medical Care in Białystok 68
10.3 Money Matters and Currency Exchange 69
10.4 Local Etiquette and Cultural Tips 70
10.5 Sustainable Travel Practices 71
Chapter 11: Useful Resources 72
11.1 Maps and City Guide Apps 73
11.2 Tourist Information Centers 74
11.3 Recommended Books and Websites 75
11.4 Contacts for Guided Tours and Excursions 77

Bialystok Travel Guide 2025
Experience Bialystok: A Traveler's Guide to the City's Best Kept Secrets

ALBERT SALVAGE

Copyright 2024 Albert Salvage.

All right reserved. No part of this publication may be reproduced, stored in a retrieval system, or transmitted in any form or by any means, electronic, mechanical, photocopying, recording, or otherwise, without prior written permission of the copyright owner.

Chapter 1: Welcome to Białystok

1.1 Introduction to Białystok

Białystok, the largest city in northeastern Poland, serves as a vibrant, culturally rich hub nestled within the lush and scenic Podlasie region. Known for its stunning architecture, including Baroque masterpieces like the famous Branicki Palace, Białystok reflects centuries of historical events and cultural blending, a unique combination that sets it apart as a significant destination. The city is home to around 300,000 residents and is the capital of the Podlaskie Voivodeship, an area renowned for its natural beauty, including extensive forests, nature reserves, and the UNESCO-listed Białowieża Forest.

The city's cultural landscape is shaped by influences from Polish, Belarusian, Jewish, Tatar, and Lithuanian communities, creating a rich tapestry of traditions, languages, and religious practices. Białystok has transformed over time into a modern, bustling city with a youthful, artistic energy, evident in its vibrant festivals, contemporary art installations, and energetic café culture. Visitors are greeted by a mix of old-world charm and innovative modernity, where historical buildings stand alongside trendy eateries, artisan shops, and bustling markets. In Białystok, every corner tells a story, making it an ideal destination for those looking to dive deep into history while enjoying the amenities of a modern city.

The city's charm also lies in its approachable scale, which allows travelers to explore its many attractions without feeling overwhelmed. The friendly atmosphere, combined with a reasonable cost of living compared to other European cities, makes Białystok an appealing choice for those seeking a memorable and immersive experience in Poland's northeastern region.

1.2 A Brief History of Białystok

Białystok's history is long and multifaceted, marked by prosperity, growth, and, at times, significant challenges. The first mentions of Białystok date back to the 15th century, when it was a small settlement within the Grand Duchy of Lithuania. However, its transformation into a prominent city began in the 18th century under the leadership of Jan Klemens Branicki, a powerful Polish nobleman who was instrumental in shaping Białystok's architectural and cultural landscape. Branicki, often regarded as the "Polish Versailles" for his opulent palace and gardens, invested in the city by building schools, hospitals, and other institutions, inviting artists and scholars to settle there and create a thriving cultural center.

The 19th century brought industrial development, with Białystok emerging as a prominent textile manufacturing hub, earning it the nickname "Manchester of the North." The city attracted a diverse workforce, including a large Jewish community that played an essential role in the city's cultural and economic life. By the early 20th century, Białystok's population had grown significantly, with Jewish, Polish, Russian, and Belarusian communities coexisting and contributing to the city's unique identity.

However, the tragedies of World War II brought irreversible changes to Białystok. The Holocaust and occupation led to the destruction of much of the Jewish community, which had been a vibrant and integral part of the city's social fabric. After the war, Białystok rebuilt itself, evolving into a modern city while still honoring its diverse history. Today, visitors can explore this complex past through its museums, monuments, and preserved historical sites, offering a poignant reminder of the city's resilience and cultural significance.

1.3 Geographical Overview

Białystok is located near Poland's eastern border, approximately 200 kilometers (124 miles) from Warsaw. The city sits on the banks of the Biała River, which gives Białystok its name, meaning "white river." This geographical position places Białystok in the heart of the Podlasie region, an area renowned for its natural landscapes, which include forests, lakes, and rolling hills. The proximity to Białowieża Forest, one of Europe's last primeval forests and home to the rare European bison, makes Białystok an ideal base for nature lovers and eco-tourists.

Białystok's urban landscape is characterized by green spaces and parks that provide a refreshing contrast to its historical buildings and modern structures. Zwierzyniecki Park and Planty Park are two prominent examples, offering scenic walking paths, vibrant flower displays, and recreational areas for residents and visitors alike. The city's layout is compact and pedestrian-friendly, with a central area that houses most of the major attractions, making it easy for travelers to explore on foot or by bike.

Beyond Białystok, the Podlasie region offers a wealth of natural and cultural treasures. The Narew and Biebrza National Parks are nearby, providing opportunities for bird-watching, kayaking, and hiking through some of Poland's most scenic and biodiverse areas. This unique blend of urban and natural landscapes makes Białystok an appealing destination for both cultural exploration and outdoor adventure.

1.4 Białystok's Climate and Best Times to Visit

Białystok experiences a temperate continental climate, characterized by distinct seasons that make each visit unique. Summers in Białystok are generally warm and pleasant, with temperatures ranging from 18°C to 25°C (64°F to 77°F), making it an ideal time for exploring outdoor attractions like Branicki Palace Gardens or embarking on day trips to nearby forests and nature reserves. The summer months, particularly June to August, are also packed with cultural events and festivals, making it a lively time to visit.

Autumn is a picturesque season in Białystok, with vibrant foliage transforming the city's parks and green spaces into a stunning palette of reds, oranges, and yellows. Temperatures during this season range from 5°C to 15°C (41°F to 59°F), which is comfortable for sightseeing and outdoor activities. Autumn is also an excellent time to visit the Białowieża Forest, where the golden leaves and crisp air make for an enchanting experience.

Winter in Białystok can be cold, with temperatures often dipping below freezing. While it may not be the ideal season for everyone, winter brings a unique charm to the city, particularly during the holiday season, when festive decorations and snow-covered streets create a cozy, enchanting atmosphere. Spring is mild and refreshing, with blooming flowers and budding trees adding color to the cityscape. Temperatures in spring range from 10°C to 18°C (50°F to 64°F), making it a pleasant time to explore Białystok's parks, botanical gardens, and outdoor markets.

Each season offers a different perspective of the city, so visitors can choose the best time to visit based on their preferences and the experiences they seek.

1.5 Language, Currency, and Practical Tips

Polish is the official language spoken in Białystok, and while English is increasingly common among younger generations and in tourist areas, learning a few basic Polish phrases can greatly enhance the travel experience. Most public transportation, menus in popular restaurants, and tourist information centers provide English translations, so language is generally not a significant barrier for visitors.

The currency used in Białystok is the Polish złoty (PLN), with exchange rates that are typically favorable for travelers from Western Europe and North America. It's advisable to carry a small amount of cash for local markets, small shops, and rural areas outside the city, although most hotels, restaurants, and larger establishments accept credit cards.

For transportation within Białystok, public buses are the primary mode and are efficient and affordable. The city also offers bike-sharing programs and pedestrian-friendly paths, making it easy for visitors to get around. When visiting religious or historical sites, it's recommended to dress modestly as a sign of respect, particularly in places of worship. Additionally, Białystok's residents appreciate environmentally conscious travelers, so practicing sustainable habits, such as recycling and using public transport, is encouraged.

Chapter 2: Getting to and Around Białystok

2.1 Transportation to Białystok

Białystok's location near Poland's eastern border makes it a convenient starting point for exploring the entire Podlaskie region as well as nearby destinations in Belarus and Lithuania. Despite its relative distance from major cities like Warsaw, Białystok is easily accessible by various transportation methods, allowing for flexible travel planning.

2.1.1 By Plane

Although Białystok does not have its own international airport, several options make flying to the region relatively simple. The nearest major airport is Warsaw Chopin Airport (WAW), located around 200 kilometers (124 miles) away. As Poland's busiest airport, Warsaw Chopin offers flights to and from many international destinations, including major European cities, North America, and Asia. From Warsaw, travelers can reach Białystok by train, bus, or car, with the journey taking roughly two to three hours depending on the mode of transportation.

Another option is Warsaw-Modlin Airport (WMI), a smaller hub that primarily serves low-cost carriers. Travelers flying into Modlin will find budget-friendly options, particularly with carriers like Ryanair, but should note that getting to Białystok will require additional travel time and transfers. Other airport alternatives include Lublin Airport (LUZ) and Olsztyn-Mazury Airport (SZY), but these are more limited in terms of international connections.

For ease and convenience, most visitors choose to fly into Warsaw and then complete the final leg of the journey by train, which offers a comfortable and scenic route through the Polish countryside.

2.1.2 By Train

Traveling by train is one of the most popular and efficient ways to reach Białystok. Poland's rail network is well-connected and generally reliable, providing frequent connections from Warsaw to Białystok. The route from Warsaw Central Station to Białystok takes about two hours on an InterCity express train, which offers modern amenities such as air-conditioning, Wi-Fi, and food services. Ticket prices for express trains are reasonable and can be even more affordable if booked in advance.

Regional trains are also available and offer a slightly longer, yet often more scenic journey, taking around three hours. These trains are less expensive than express services and provide a comfortable alternative for budget-conscious travelers. Both types of trains arrive at Białystok Główny (Białystok Main Station), conveniently located near the city center.

In addition to Warsaw, Białystok is connected by train to other major Polish cities, including Gdańsk, Kraków, and Wrocław, making it easy to include Białystok in a broader travel itinerary. For travelers interested in cross-border exploration, Białystok's rail connections to Lithuania are expanding, and there are plans to increase direct routes to Vilnius.

2.1.3 By Bus and Car

Bus travel is another convenient and economical option for getting to Białystok, especially for those arriving from smaller Polish cities or looking to save on travel costs. Multiple bus companies, including FlixBus and PKS, operate routes between Warsaw and Białystok, with frequent departures throughout the day. The journey typically takes around three hours, with prices that are generally lower than those of train tickets. Buses are comfortable, equipped with Wi-Fi and restrooms, and many have reclining seats, making for a pleasant ride.

Traveling by car allows for a more flexible schedule and provides an opportunity to explore the beautiful Podlasie countryside at your own pace. The drive from Warsaw to Białystok takes approximately two and a half hours via National Road 8, a well-maintained highway that offers a direct route to the city. Visitors who prefer to rent a car should note that while major highways are easy to navigate, rural roads may require more caution, especially during winter.

For visitors interested in cross-border trips, car travel also makes it feasible to visit nearby regions in Belarus and Lithuania. However, if you plan to cross into Belarus, you'll need to check visa requirements and border regulations, as they differ from those of EU member states.

2.2 Public Transportation within the City

Once in Białystok, getting around is straightforward thanks to an efficient public transportation system primarily composed of buses operated by KPK Białystok. The bus network covers nearly every corner of the city, making it easy to reach attractions, dining spots, and shopping areas. Buses run frequently from early morning until late evening, with certain routes offering limited night services. Tickets can be purchased at kiosks, directly from the driver, or through mobile apps.

Białystok's public transport system uses a zone-based fare structure, with single-ride tickets, day passes, and multi-day options available. For tourists planning to explore several neighborhoods, a 24-hour pass or weekend pass is often the most cost-effective choice. The buses are modern, clean, and many are accessible for passengers with disabilities.

2.3 Renting a Car or Bicycle

For travelers who want more freedom to explore, renting a car in Białystok is a convenient option. Rental agencies are available near the main train station and the city center, with both international companies like Avis and Hertz, as well as local providers offering competitive rates. Car rentals provide easy access to outlying natural areas and nearby national parks, such as Białowieża Forest and Biebrza National Park, where public transportation options may be limited.

For an eco-friendly and leisurely way to explore Białystok's compact city center, consider renting a bicycle. The city operates BiKeR, a bike-sharing program with stations across major points of interest. Renting a bike is simple and affordable; after registering through the BiKeR app, users can unlock and ride bikes at any docking station, returning them to any other location when finished. Biking is particularly popular in the warmer months and allows visitors to experience the city's scenic parks and green spaces more closely.

2.4 Walking Tours and Exploring on Foot

Białystok's compact city layout makes it a pedestrian-friendly destination. Most of the city's historical landmarks, cultural sites, and popular attractions are within walking distance of each other, especially in the city center. The pedestrian-friendly main square and surrounding streets are perfect for a leisurely stroll, where visitors can admire Białystok's unique architectural mix, sample local cafes, and soak up the city's relaxed atmosphere.

For those interested in a guided experience, several companies offer walking tours that focus on Białystok's history, architecture, and multicultural heritage. Guided walking tours typically last two to three hours and include stops at key attractions like Branicki Palace, Białystok Market Square, and the Orthodox Church of St. Nicholas. Specialized tours also highlight the city's Jewish heritage, street art, and hidden gems that might otherwise go unnoticed.

Self-guided tours are also popular, and maps with suggested routes are available at the city's main tourist information centers. The flexibility of exploring Białystok on foot allows visitors to discover lesser-known spots, interact with locals, and experience the city's authentic charm.

Białystok's accessibility and ease of navigation make it an ideal destination for visitors seeking both convenience and rich experiences. Whether arriving by train, bus, car, or foot, the city's well-planned transportation options provide everything needed to explore its unique mix of history, culture, and natural beauty. Each mode of transport offers distinct advantages, allowing travelers to tailor their journey to suit their interests and preferences.

With these transportation options covered, the guide equips readers to comfortably navigate their way to and within Białystok, ready for the adventures and discoveries that await.

Chapter 3: Top Attractions in Białystok

Białystok is a city of rich history, diverse culture, and scenic beauty, where centuries-old palaces and churches blend seamlessly with modern arts and entertainment venues. Visitors to Białystok will find an array of attractions that showcase the city's storied past, its deep-rooted multiculturalism, and its vibrant, evolving arts scene. Here's a guide to the top attractions that make Białystok a compelling destination for travelers.

3.1 Branicki Palace and Gardens

Often referred to as the "Polish Versailles," the Branicki Palace is one of Białystok's most iconic landmarks and a must-see for any visitor. Originally built in the 17th century by Stefan Mikołaj Branicki, the palace was later transformed into a grand Baroque residence by his son, Jan Klemens Branicki, a Polish nobleman and one of the wealthiest magnates of his time. The palace's design was inspired by the French Versailles and was intended to be a residence worthy of royal stature, a goal reflected in its opulent architecture and meticulously manicured gardens.

The Branicki Palace complex includes ornate gates, a grand courtyard, and beautifully maintained gardens featuring fountains, sculptures, and lush greenery. The gardens, laid out in the formal French style, are ideal for a leisurely stroll, especially in spring and summer when the flowers are in full bloom. Visitors can also explore parts of the palace's interior, where they'll find period furnishings, portraits, and exhibitions showcasing the history of the Branicki family and the city of Białystok. Today, the palace houses the Medical University of Białystok, which maintains the building's historical character while adding a modern touch to its traditional charm.

3.2 Białystok Historical Museum

Located in a restored historic townhouse, the Białystok Historical Museum offers a glimpse into the city's past, with exhibits that cover everything from its multicultural heritage to its industrial development in the 19th and 20th centuries. The museum's collection includes artifacts from Białystok's Polish, Jewish, Russian, and Belarusian communities, reflecting the city's diverse cultural influences. The museum's exhibitions cover topics like Białystok's role as a textile industry hub, its Jewish heritage, and the impact of World War II on the local community.

One of the museum's highlights is the section dedicated to Białystok's Jewish heritage, which was a significant part of the city's identity before the Holocaust. This part of the museum honors the memory of Białystok's Jewish residents and provides insight into their contributions to the city's development. Temporary exhibitions also showcase local artists, historical photography, and interactive displays that bring Białystok's history to life for visitors of all ages.

3.3 Podlasie Opera and Philharmonic

The Podlasie Opera and Philharmonic is the largest cultural institution in northeastern Poland and a major center for music, theater, and performing arts in Białystok. Opened in 2012, this state-of-the-art venue features a main concert hall, a chamber hall, and an outdoor amphitheater, each designed to provide top-notch acoustics and viewing experiences. The opera house is an architectural marvel, with a sleek, modern design that incorporates natural materials like glass and wood, blending seamlessly with its surroundings.

The Podlasie Opera and Philharmonic hosts a wide range of performances, from operas and ballets to symphony concerts and theatrical productions. It also serves as the venue for several annual events, such as the Białystok International Opera Festival, which attracts renowned artists and ensembles from around the world. For travelers interested in the arts, attending a performance here is a wonderful way to experience Białystok's cultural scene in an elegant and immersive setting.

3.4 St. Roch's Basilica

An architectural standout in Białystok, St. Roch's Basilica is a unique modernist church built in the 20th century. Commissioned by Poland's government to celebrate the nation's independence after World War I, the church was designed by the architect Oskar Sosnowski, whose plans incorporated traditional elements with avant-garde shapes and motifs. The basilica's striking white facade, tall tower, and intricate reliefs make it an impressive sight that stands out on Białystok's skyline.

The interior of St. Roch's Basilica is equally captivating, with high ceilings, colorful stained glass windows, and a minimalist design that exudes a sense of peace and reverence. The church's location atop a hill provides excellent views of the surrounding city, making it a popular spot for both sightseeing and quiet reflection. St. Roch's Basilica is not only a place of worship but also a monument to Polish independence and resilience, holding deep historical and national significance.

3.5 Białystok Market Square and City Hall

The Market Square (Rynek Kościuszki) is the heart of Białystok's historic district and a bustling hub of local activity. Lined with cafes, restaurants, and boutiques, the square offers a lively atmosphere where locals and tourists gather to socialize, dine, and shop. At the center of the square stands the Białystok City Hall, a Baroque-style building that dates back to the 18th century. Although it was originally used as a town hall, the building now houses the Białystok Museum of Art, where visitors can explore exhibits on local art, crafts, and cultural history.

The Market Square is also a popular location for festivals, open-air concerts, and seasonal markets, including a Christmas market where visitors can find unique gifts and sample holiday treats. The area's pedestrian-friendly layout makes it perfect for a leisurely stroll, and its vibrant café scene offers ample opportunities for people-watching and soaking in the local culture. Whether visiting during the day or evening, the Market Square is a quintessential Białystok experience.

3.6 Lubomirski Palace

Located near the center of Białystok, the Lubomirski Palace is a historical residence that once belonged to the influential Lubomirski family. While it may not be as grand as the Branicki Palace, Lubomirski Palace holds a charm of its own, with Baroque architectural elements and a serene garden that makes it a peaceful retreat. The palace has undergone renovations to restore its original elegance, and today it serves as a venue for cultural events, exhibitions, and educational programs.

The palace grounds include a small park where visitors can enjoy a quiet walk, surrounded by statues, fountains, and manicured landscaping. The interior, while not fully open to the public, occasionally hosts special exhibitions that provide insight into the lives of the Polish nobility and the architectural styles of the time. For those interested in Białystok's noble heritage, a visit to Lubomirski Palace is a pleasant addition to the itinerary.

3.7 Parks and Green Spaces

Białystok is known for its abundant green spaces, which offer residents and visitors alike a chance to relax, exercise, and enjoy the natural beauty of the Podlasie region. Planty Park, located near Branicki Palace, is one of the city's most popular parks, featuring walking paths, flower beds, and benches where visitors can unwind in a tranquil setting. The park is also home to several sculptures and art installations, adding an artistic touch to the natural surroundings.

Another notable green space is Zwierzyniecki Park, a wooded area that provides a more rustic, natural experience. The park includes trails for jogging, cycling, and leisurely walks, as well as playgrounds for children and picnic spots for families. Zwierzyniecki Park is a great destination for nature lovers, and its proximity to the city center makes it easily accessible for those looking to escape the urban bustle.

3.8 Day Trips and Nearby Attractions

For travelers looking to explore beyond the city limits, Białystok offers a variety of day trip options to nearby attractions. The UNESCO-listed Białowieża Forest, located about an hour's drive from Białystok, is one of Europe's last remaining primeval forests and home to the endangered European bison. The forest offers guided tours, hiking trails, and opportunities for wildlife observation, making it a popular destination for nature enthusiasts.

Another nearby attraction is Tykocin, a charming town known for its well-preserved Baroque architecture and historic Jewish heritage. Tykocin's main square, 17th-century synagogue, and Tykocin Castle are just a few of the highlights that make this town a worthwhile day trip from Białystok.

For those interested in history and nature, the Narew National Park and Biebrza National Park are also within easy reach of Białystok. These parks offer unique wetland ecosystems, bird-watching opportunities, and serene landscapes that showcase the natural diversity of the Podlasie region.

Białystok's attractions are a testament to its rich history, cultural diversity, and dedication to preserving its natural beauty. From the grandeur of Branicki Palace to the serene landscapes of its parks, the city provides a wealth of experiences for visitors of all interests. Whether exploring historical landmarks, enjoying the arts, or venturing into the surrounding countryside, Białystok offers something for everyone.

Chapter 4: Art and Culture

Białystok is a cultural crossroads where Eastern and Western influences meet, creating a vibrant, eclectic art scene. The city's diverse cultural heritage, shaped by Polish, Jewish, Belarusian, and Russian traditions, is reflected in its arts, festivals, and architecture. Whether you're an art enthusiast, a history buff, or a lover of live performances, Białystok offers a range of cultural attractions and events that showcase its unique heritage and contemporary creative spirit.

4.1 Art Galleries and Museums

Białystok's art galleries and museums provide insight into the region's artistic evolution, from traditional folk art to contemporary works.

4.1.1 Białystok Art Gallery

Białystok Art Gallery is a prominent venue for contemporary art, showcasing works by local and international artists. The gallery hosts rotating exhibitions, which include paintings, sculptures, installations, and multimedia works, providing visitors with a look at both the Polish and global art scenes. The gallery also organizes workshops and lectures, making it an engaging space for art lovers and students alike. Its focus on modern themes and innovative expressions makes the Białystok Art Gallery a must-visit for anyone interested in contemporary Polish art.

4.1.2 Museum of Folk Culture

Located just outside the city, the Museum of Folk Culture in Wasilków offers a fascinating look at the traditional arts and crafts of the Podlasie region. This open-air museum features a collection of reconstructed wooden cottages, barns, and windmills, each furnished with period-appropriate items that show what life was like in rural Podlasie. Exhibits include traditional crafts, such as weaving, pottery, and woodworking, along with seasonal events where local artisans demonstrate these skills. The museum is particularly popular among families and those interested in Poland's rural heritage and is a wonderful way to experience the cultural roots of the region.

4.2 The Białystok Theater Scene

Białystok's theater scene is a reflection of its historical diversity and contemporary energy, with several notable venues offering a range of performances.

Białystok Puppet Theater

One of the oldest and most respected puppet theaters in Poland, the Białystok Puppet Theater is renowned for its captivating performances for audiences of all ages. The theater's repertoire includes traditional puppet shows, experimental performances, and adaptations of classic literature, using puppetry as a unique medium for storytelling. The theater's skilled puppeteers bring each performance to life with precision and creativity, making it a memorable experience for visitors.

The theater also organizes the biennial International Puppet Festival, attracting performers from around the world to showcase their talents in this art form. Whether traveling with children or as an adult, a visit to the Białystok Puppet Theater provides a unique look at an often-overlooked aspect of performing arts.

Aleksander Węgierko Drama Theater

Named after its founder, the Aleksander Węgierko Drama Theater is one of the most prestigious theaters in Białystok. Known for its innovative productions and talented ensemble, the theater offers a diverse range of performances, including dramas, comedies, and modern adaptations of classical works. The building itself, with its neoclassical architecture and elegant interiors, is a landmark in the city center. Attending a performance here provides visitors with an opportunity to enjoy high-quality Polish theater in a beautiful setting.

4.3 Annual Festivals and Events

Białystok's calendar is filled with festivals that celebrate everything from theater to music and cultural heritage. These events offer a great opportunity to experience the city's lively atmosphere and engage with its artistic community.

4.3.1 International Theater Festival

The Białystok International Theater Festival is a highlight of the city's cultural calendar, bringing together theater companies and performers from across Europe and beyond. Held annually, the festival showcases a wide range of performances, from traditional plays and puppet shows to experimental theater. The event also includes workshops, discussions, and meet-and-greet sessions with the performers, offering an immersive experience for theater enthusiasts. The festival's emphasis on diversity and artistic innovation makes it a significant cultural event that attracts audiences from all over Poland.

4.3.2 Jewish Culture Festival

The Jewish Culture Festival in Białystok celebrates the city's rich Jewish heritage, honoring the contributions of the Jewish community to Białystok's cultural and social fabric. The festival features concerts, film screenings, lectures, and guided tours that explore the city's Jewish history and architecture. Highlights of the festival include klezmer music performances, exhibitions of Jewish art, and traditional dance workshops. This event serves as both a commemoration and a celebration, bringing together people of all backgrounds to appreciate and learn about Jewish culture.

4.3.3 Białystok Days Celebration

Every summer, the city hosts the Białystok Days, a multi-day event celebrating the city's history, achievements, and community spirit. Białystok Days feature parades, outdoor concerts, art exhibitions, and local food vendors, creating a festive atmosphere in the heart of the city. Residents and visitors alike take to the streets to enjoy live music, sample regional dishes, and explore the various cultural displays. This festival reflects the pride and vibrancy of Białystok, and for visitors, it's a fantastic way to experience the local culture and sense of community.

4.4 The Jewish Heritage and Synagogues

Białystok's Jewish heritage is a profound part of its identity, as the city was once home to a large and thriving Jewish community. While much of this community was lost during the Holocaust, there are still several sites and initiatives that honor Białystok's Jewish legacy.

Synagogue Memorial and Former Jewish District

One of the most poignant reminders of Białystok's Jewish heritage is the Synagogue Memorial, located on the site of the former Great Synagogue, which was destroyed during World War II. The memorial is a solemn tribute to the Jewish residents who lost their lives during the Holocaust and serves as a place of reflection and remembrance. The surrounding area, which once formed the center of Białystok's Jewish district, is filled with historical markers and plaques that provide insight into the lives of the city's Jewish residents.

Cultural Programs and Educational Tours

Several organizations in Białystok offer educational tours that focus on Jewish history and heritage, providing an in-depth look at the community's contributions to the city. These tours typically include visits to key sites, such as the Jewish cemetery and the remains of the ghetto wall, as well as personal stories and accounts that bring Białystok's Jewish past to life. In addition to guided tours, the city also hosts cultural programs and events dedicated to Jewish heritage, ensuring that this important part of Białystok's history is not forgotten.

Jewish Cemetery

Established in the early 19th century, the Jewish Cemetery in Białystok is one of the few remaining relics of the once-thriving Jewish community. Although many of the gravestones were damaged or destroyed during the war, the cemetery has since been partially restored and is open to visitors. Wandering through the rows of graves, visitors can reflect on the city's history and the lasting legacy of the Jewish community in Białystok.

Białystok's art and cultural scene is a unique blend of history, tradition, and innovation. From its theaters and galleries to its festivals and heritage sites, the city offers a wealth of experiences for those eager to learn about its diverse cultural tapestry. Whether you're exploring the works of contemporary artists, attending a puppet show, or participating in a traditional festival, Białystok's art and culture scene provides a deeper understanding of the city's identity and the resilience of its people.

Chapter 5: The Culinary Scene in Białystok

Białystok's culinary landscape is a reflection of the city's diverse cultural heritage, combining flavors and influences from Polish, Jewish, Lithuanian, Belarusian, and Ukrainian cuisines. Known for hearty dishes and farm-fresh ingredients, Białystok offers visitors a chance to experience both traditional Polish fare and creative modern takes on regional recipes. The city's dining scene features everything from cozy, family-owned eateries to upscale restaurants, as well as bustling markets where you can find local delicacies and fresh produce. In this guide, we'll take a closer look at the must-try dishes, dining venues, and culinary experiences that make Białystok's food scene truly special.

5.1 Traditional Polish Dishes to Try

Polish cuisine is known for its hearty, flavorful dishes that are perfect for the region's cooler climate. In Białystok, visitors can enjoy an array of traditional Polish dishes, many of which have been influenced by the city's multicultural history. Here are some local specialties to try:

5.1.1 Pierogi

Pierogi are perhaps the most iconic Polish dish, and you'll find them served at nearly every restaurant in Białystok. These dumplings are made from dough and can be filled with a variety of ingredients, from savory options like potatoes, cheese, and mushrooms to sweet fillings like blueberries or cherries. In Białystok, many restaurants offer their own unique twists on pierogi, often featuring regional ingredients or innovative flavor combinations.

5.1.2 Bigos

Known as the "hunter's stew," bigos is a hearty dish made with a mixture of sauerkraut, fresh cabbage, various meats (such as pork, sausage, and bacon), and mushrooms. Traditionally, bigos is slow-cooked over several days, allowing the flavors to meld together. It's a comforting, filling meal that's perfect for cold weather, and it's a favorite in Białystok's traditional eateries. Each restaurant has its own variation of bigos, with some adding local ingredients for a unique twist.

5.1.3 Żurek

Żurek is a traditional Polish soup made from fermented rye flour, which gives it a slightly sour flavor. It's typically served with sausages, boiled eggs, and sometimes potatoes, creating a rich and satisfying dish. In Białystok, Żurek is often served in a hollowed-out bread bowl, adding a rustic touch to this beloved soup. Many restaurants offer Żurek as a starter, and it's especially popular during Easter celebrations.

5.1.4 Kopytka

Kopytka, or Polish potato dumplings, are similar to Italian gnocchi and are often served with a variety of toppings, including butter, herbs, cheese, or fried onions. These dumplings are soft and slightly chewy, making them a comforting and filling side dish. Kopytka are popular in traditional Polish restaurants in Białystok, and they're often paired with dishes like stews or meat dishes.

5.2 Popular Local Restaurants

Białystok's dining scene includes a mix of traditional Polish eateries, modern bistros, and international restaurants, offering something for every taste. Here are a few popular dining spots to consider:

5.2.1 Polish Cuisine

Restauracja Esperanto – Named after the international language invented by Białystok's own Ludwik Zamenhof, Restauracja Esperanto offers a mix of traditional Polish dishes with a modern twist. The restaurant's menu features favorites like pierogi, bigos, and duck with apples, all made with fresh, locally sourced ingredients. The ambiance is cozy yet elegant, making it a great spot for both casual dining and special occasions.

Kafejeto – This quaint cafe and restaurant serves a range of traditional Polish dishes with a focus on homemade flavors. Kafejeto's menu changes with the seasons, offering dishes that highlight local ingredients. The atmosphere is warm and welcoming, with rustic decor and friendly staff, making it a favorite among locals and visitors alike.

5.2.2 International Flavors

Kuchnia Otwarta – For those craving international cuisine, Kuchnia Otwarta offers an eclectic menu with influences from Italian, French, and Mediterranean cuisines. The restaurant uses fresh, seasonal ingredients and places an emphasis on presentation. The open kitchen concept allows diners to watch the chefs at work, creating an engaging and immersive dining experience.

Pizza Express Białystok – Pizza Express offers high-quality, wood-fired pizza with a range of toppings to suit any taste. While pizza is the main attraction here, the restaurant also serves salads, pastas, and desserts, making it a great option for families and groups. The casual, vibrant atmosphere makes it a popular choice for a relaxed meal.

5.2.3 Vegetarian and Vegan Options

Piękna i Bestia – A beloved spot for vegetarian and vegan cuisine, Piękna i Bestia offers a variety of plant-based dishes made with fresh, organic ingredients. The menu includes options like vegan pierogi, mushroom risotto, and delicious smoothie bowls. The restaurant's commitment to sustainability and its creative approach to traditional Polish dishes make it a must-visit for vegetarian and vegan travelers.

Wegańska Uczta – Specializing in vegan and vegetarian comfort food, Wegańska Uczta has a menu filled with hearty, flavorful dishes. From vegan burgers and wraps to creative salads and soups, there's something to satisfy every craving. The atmosphere is laid-back, and the restaurant's focus on ethical and environmentally friendly practices resonates with many visitors.

5.3 Local Markets and Specialty Foods

Exploring Białystok's markets is a fantastic way to experience the region's culinary culture firsthand. Local markets are filled with fresh produce, artisanal products, and regional specialties, offering visitors a taste of traditional Podlasie flavors.

5.3.1 Białystok Central Market

Białystok Central Market is a bustling marketplace where vendors sell fresh fruits, vegetables, dairy products, meats, and more. The market is especially known for its selection of local cheeses, smoked meats, and pickled vegetables, all of which are staples in Polish cuisine. Many of the products are sourced from nearby farms, ensuring freshness and high quality. Visitors can sample a variety of foods as they browse, making it a great way to discover new flavors and support local producers.

5.3.2 Specialty Food Shops

In addition to the Central Market, Białystok has several specialty food shops that offer unique, locally made products. These shops often carry items like artisanal honey, locally brewed beer, and specialty pastries. Some popular local treats include "sękacz" (a layered cake cooked over an open flame) and "podlaski chleba" (regional bread). These shops provide a chance to take a piece of Białystok's culinary heritage home with you, whether as a souvenir or a gift.

5.4 Breweries and Nightlife

Białystok's nightlife offers a lively selection of bars, pubs, and breweries, each with its own distinct atmosphere and range of drinks.

5.4.1 Local Breweries

Białystok is home to a few local breweries that produce a variety of craft beers, often inspired by regional flavors.

Browar Gloger – This local brewery takes its name from Polish ethnographer Zygmunt Gloger and specializes in craft beers that reflect the flavors of the Podlasie region. With an assortment of pilsners, IPAs, and seasonal brews, Browar Gloger offers something for every beer enthusiast. Visitors can sample beers at the brewery's taproom, which often hosts tasting events and brewery tours.

Pub Kaktusik – Known for its cozy atmosphere and extensive beer selection, Pub Kaktusik is a favorite among locals. The pub features a rotating menu of Polish and international craft beers, including several varieties from local brewers. With live music and a friendly crowd, Pub Kaktusik is a great place to unwind after a day of exploring.

5.4.2 Cocktail Bars and Lounges

For those seeking a more refined experience, Białystok offers a selection of cocktail bars and lounges where you can enjoy expertly crafted drinks in a relaxed setting.

Mała Czarna – This upscale bar is known for its unique cocktails made with local ingredients, as well as its chic, modern ambiance. The bartenders are skilled at creating custom drinks based on individual tastes, making each visit a unique experience. Mała Czarna's dedication to quality and creativity has earned it a loyal following among both locals and visitors.

Bar Stary Browar – Housed in a historic brewery building, Bar Stary Browar combines the charm of old Białystok with a modern twist. The bar serves a variety of local beers and spirits, along with a creative menu of cocktails inspired by Polish and regional flavors. The vintage decor and warm atmosphere make it a popular choice for both casual and special occasions.

5.5 Food and Cultural Events

Białystok hosts several food-focused events and festivals that celebrate the region's culinary heritage and showcase local talent.

5.5.1 Podlasie Tastes Festival

The Podlasie Tastes Festival is a multi-day event that takes place annually, celebrating the traditional flavors of the Podlasie region. During the festival, local chefs and artisans set up stalls in the city center, offering everything from homemade sausages and smoked fish to artisanal cheeses and pastries. The festival also includes cooking demonstrations, food tastings, and live entertainment, creating a festive atmosphere for food lovers of all ages.

Białystok's culinary scene offers visitors a delicious journey through the flavors and traditions of the Podlasie region. From traditional Polish dishes to innovative modern cuisine, the city's restaurants, markets, and festivals provide endless opportunities to explore and indulge. Whether you're a food enthusiast, a curious traveler, or simply looking to enjoy a memorable meal, Białystok's food culture is sure to leave a lasting impression.

Chapter 6: Outdoor Activities and Nature

Białystok, known for its lush greenery and proximity to beautiful natural landscapes, offers a wealth of outdoor activities for those who want to explore the region's unique ecosystem and experience its peaceful beauty. Białystok's parks, forests, and rivers provide the perfect setting for hiking, biking, and even wildlife watching. This chapter will guide you through the best outdoor experiences Białystok has to offer, from scenic nature trails to must-visit green spaces and outdoor recreational areas.

6.1 Hiking and Nature Trails

Białystok and the surrounding region are known for their hiking trails, many of which wind through forests, alongside rivers, and through protected nature reserves. For outdoor enthusiasts, these trails offer the opportunity to enjoy the area's natural beauty up close.

6.1.1 Białowieża Forest

One of the most famous nature destinations in the area is Białowieża Forest, a UNESCO World Heritage Site and one of Europe's last primeval forests. Located just a short drive from Białystok, this ancient forest spans the border between Poland and Belarus and is home to the European bison, Europe's largest land mammal. Hikers can explore a variety of trails within the forest, with options ranging from easy, family-friendly paths to more challenging routes that go deeper into the wilderness.

- **Zebra Zubrów Trail** – This trail leads visitors through some of the most beautiful areas of Białowieża Forest, including spots where bison can often be spotted. The trail is well-marked and takes around 2–3 hours to complete, making it a manageable choice for casual hikers and families.

- **Nature Reserve Trails** – For a more immersive experience, several trails lead into protected nature reserves within the forest. These trails are best accessed with a guide, as they go deeper into the forest where rare species of plants and animals can be observed.

6.1.2 Narew National Park

Located along the Narew River, Narew National Park is a paradise for nature lovers. The park features unique waterways and marshlands, making it a popular spot for bird-watching, hiking, and kayaking.

Known as the "Polish Amazon" due to its winding rivers, the park's trails include:

- **Boardwalk Trails** – The park has several boardwalk paths that take visitors through wetlands and over streams, offering beautiful views and the chance to spot birds, frogs, and other wildlife. The boardwalks are accessible and family-friendly, making them an ideal choice for all ages.

- **Educational Trails** – Narew National Park also has trails specifically designed for educational purposes, with signs and information boards explaining the local flora and fauna, the significance of the wetland ecosystem, and the importance of conservation efforts.

6.2 Biking Routes and Rentals

Biking is a popular way to explore Białystok and the surrounding region, as the city has well-developed bike paths and rental options that make it easy to get around. Several bike routes cater to both beginners and more experienced cyclists.

6.2.1 Green Velo Trail

The Green Velo Trail is a cycling route that stretches across eastern Poland, passing through Białystok and offering cyclists a scenic way to explore the area. This long-distance route includes designated sections for bike-friendly accommodations, repair stations, and viewpoints. The trail covers a variety of landscapes, including forests, rivers, and villages, allowing cyclists to experience the natural beauty and local culture of Podlasie.

6.2.2 City Bike Rentals and Trails

Białystok's city bike-sharing program, BiKeR, offers convenient rental options for short trips around the city. Białystok has several designated bike lanes, and popular cycling routes include the trails around Zwierzyniec Park and Branicki Palace Gardens. Renting a bike for a few hours is an affordable and eco-friendly way to explore Białystok's main attractions at your own pace.

6.2.3 Regional Bike Trails

For those looking to venture beyond the city, several bike trails connect Białystok with nearby towns and scenic spots. These routes vary in length and difficulty, making them suitable for day trips or multi-day cycling adventures. Maps and guides are available at local tourist centers, and several companies offer guided cycling tours for those who prefer exploring in a group.

6.3 Białowieża Forest Day Trips

Białowieża Forest is a popular day trip destination from Białystok, offering visitors the chance to explore a UNESCO World Heritage Site and see the famous European bison in their natural habitat.

6.3.1 Guided Tours

For first-time visitors, a guided tour is the best way to experience Białowieża Forest. Experienced guides can share insights about the forest's ecosystem, history, and wildlife, adding depth to your visit. Guided tours typically include stops at key points of interest, such as:

- **The European Bison Reserve** – One of the highlights of Białowieża Forest is the opportunity to see European bison, a species that has been successfully reintroduced to the forest. The reserve provides a safe environment where visitors can observe these majestic animals up close while learning about conservation efforts.

- **Palace Park and Nature Museum** – Białowieża's Palace Park, designed in the English garden style, is a beautiful place to relax and enjoy the scenery. The nearby Nature Museum offers exhibits on the flora and fauna of Białowieża Forest, making it a great starting point for your visit.

6.3.2 Self-Guided Hiking and Wildlife Spotting

For those who prefer to explore independently, Białowieża Forest has several well-marked hiking trails where you can enjoy the natural beauty of the forest. Maps are available at the park entrance, and the trails range from easy walks to more challenging hikes that take you deeper into the forest.

6.4 Boat Trips and Water Sports

Białystok's rivers and lakes provide excellent opportunities for water-based activities, from kayaking and canoeing to paddleboarding. These activities offer a fun way to explore the region's natural beauty while enjoying the tranquility of the water.

6.4.1 Kayaking on the Narew River

The Narew River, with its calm, meandering waters, is ideal for kayaking. Several companies in the area offer kayak rentals and guided tours, allowing visitors to paddle through the picturesque marshlands and observe the diverse bird species that inhabit the riverbanks.

- **Popular Kayaking Routes** – One popular route for kayaking takes you from the town of Łapy to the outskirts of Białystok, passing through the scenic landscapes of Narew National Park. This route is beginner-friendly and offers plenty of spots for picnicking and bird-watching.

- **Guided Nature Kayak Tours** – For those new to kayaking or who want to learn more about the local ecosystem, guided nature tours are available. These tours typically include information on the river's flora and fauna, as well as tips for spotting wildlife.

6.4.2 Paddleboarding on Dojlidy Lagoon

Dojlidy Lagoon, located just a short drive from Białystok, is a popular spot for paddleboarding. The calm, clear waters make it an ideal place for beginners, and rental facilities are available at the beach area. Paddleboarding is a great way to enjoy the lagoon's scenic surroundings, especially during the warmer months when the water is most inviting.

6.5 Family-Friendly Outdoor Spots

For families visiting Białystok, the city and its surroundings offer several parks and outdoor attractions that are perfect for kids and parents alike.

6.5.1 Planty Park

Planty Park, located in the heart of Białystok, is a beautifully landscaped park with walking paths, playgrounds, and picnic areas. The park's central location makes it easily accessible for families, and its well-maintained paths are suitable for strollers. Kids will love the playground area, and there are plenty of benches and shady spots for parents to relax.

6.5.2 Branicki Palace Gardens

The gardens at Branicki Palace are not only a historical attraction but also a peaceful green space where families can enjoy a leisurely stroll. The gardens are filled with fountains, flowerbeds, and sculpted hedges, making them a picturesque spot for photos. Guided tours of the palace are available, and the gardens are open to the public year-round.

6.5.3 Zwierzyniec Park and Mini Zoo

Zwierzyniec Park, located just outside of Białystok, features a mini zoo where kids can see animals like deer, goats, and various bird species. The park also has several walking trails, picnic areas, and playgrounds, making it a great option for a family day out in nature. The mini zoo offers an educational experience for children, while the surrounding forest provides a peaceful environment for walking and exploring.

Białystok's outdoor activities and natural attractions make it an ideal destination for those looking to connect with nature. From the ancient forests of Białowieża to the scenic river trails and family-friendly parks, Białystok offers a diverse array of outdoor experiences that cater to all interests and skill levels. Whether you're an avid hiker, a casual cyclist, or simply looking for a peaceful spot to relax, Białystok's natural landscapes provide a refreshing escape from the hustle and bustle of city life.

Chapter 7: Accommodations in Białystok

Chapter Overview: In this chapter, we'll introduce readers to the diverse accommodation options in Białystok, from luxury hotels to cozy vacation rentals. With a range of budgets in mind, each section will detail the best places to stay based on amenities, location, and atmosphere.

7.1 Hotels in Białystok

Białystok has a selection of hotels that balance modern amenities with cultural charm. Luxury hotels near the city center often provide easy access to historic landmarks like the Branicki Palace or the Podlasie Opera and Philharmonic. These establishments generally feature well-regarded restaurants, spa services, and panoramic views of the cityscape.

Highlights:

- **Hotel Esperanto**: Known for its elegant Art Nouveau style, this hotel combines comfort with tradition. Conveniently located near city landmarks, it's perfect for travelers who want both style and proximity.

- **Royal Hotel & Spa**: This luxury option includes a full-service spa and an on-site restaurant specializing in Podlasie cuisine, making it a favorite among visitors looking to unwind.

7.2 Budget-Friendly Hostels

Travelers on a budget can find several affordable hostels around Białystok, ideal for those looking to save while still enjoying the city. These hostels are clean, friendly, and often provide communal spaces to meet other travelers. Dormitory-style accommodations, shared kitchens, and proximity to public transport make them excellent choices for budget-conscious tourists.

Popular Options:

- **Hostel Sweet Dream**: Located close to public transportation, this hostel provides a range of room types from dormitories to private rooms, along with complimentary breakfast.

- **Youth Hostel Białystok**: A favorite for young travelers, offering a friendly environment and helpful local staff who provide insights on lesser-known attractions.

7.3 Boutique Hotels and Unique Stays

For travelers seeking a unique experience, Białystok's boutique hotels and themed accommodations offer charm and local flavor. These stays often reflect the history or artistic culture of the region and may be located in renovated historical buildings or designed with creative modern flair.

Featured Stays:

- **Hotel Branicki**: A boutique hotel that embraces the city's historical roots, named after the Branicki family. Guests can expect old-world charm, antiques, and a European-style courtyard.

- **Villa Tradycja**: Known for its blend of rustic and chic design, this hotel features traditionally inspired decor and high-quality linens.

7.4 Vacation Rentals and Apartments

For those who prefer a more independent experience, Białystok has a variety of vacation rentals available. Apartments are particularly popular among families and groups, allowing for flexible schedules and often more space than traditional hotels.

Top Neighborhoods for Rentals:

- **Śródmieście**: Central, close to attractions, with access to restaurants, cafes, and shopping.

- **Bojary**: A quieter neighborhood known for its scenic streets and historic wooden houses, offering a more residential experience.

7.5 Family-Friendly Accommodation Options

Traveling with children? Many hotels and rentals in Białystok cater to families, with options like interconnected rooms, playgrounds, or even kids' clubs. Family-friendly stays provide not only comfort but also convenience for a stress-free family holiday.

Family Recommendations:

- **ApartHotel Nord**: Known for its spacious suites and playground, ideal for families wanting easy access to the city's main attractions.

- **Best Western Hotel Cristal**: With a family-oriented atmosphere and kids' menu, it's a great choice for parents seeking a comfortable stay.

Chapter 8: Shopping in Białystok

Chapter Overview: Białystok offers a diverse shopping experience that caters to all kinds of shoppers. In this chapter, we'll explore shopping malls, department stores, and local artisan shops where travelers can pick up unique souvenirs and enjoy Białystok's rich culture through its local products.

8.1 Shopping Malls and Department Stores

Białystok is home to a variety of shopping malls, perfect for travelers looking for everything from international brands to entertainment options under one roof. These malls often include restaurants, cinemas, and play areas for children, making them excellent destinations for a day out.

Highlights:

- **Galeria Jurowiecka**: One of the most popular shopping centers in Białystok, Galeria Jurowiecka has a vast selection of international and Polish brands. The mall is conveniently located near the city center and includes cafes and restaurants, ideal for a mid-shopping break.

- **Atrium Biała**: This mall is perfect for those interested in both shopping and entertainment, with a multiplex cinema, diverse dining options, and fashion stores featuring popular Polish and international brands. Atrium Biała's extensive layout also includes sections dedicated to electronics, home decor, and beauty services.

Tips for Visitors:

- **Discount Seasons**: Sales and promotions often coincide with holidays, including the end-of-year festive season, making these times great for scoring deals.

- **VAT Refunds**: Many stores allow VAT refunds for non-EU citizens. Be sure to ask about Tax-Free shopping options for additional savings.

8.2 Local Artisan Shops

For those who want a taste of Białystok's unique culture, the city's artisan shops offer one-of-a-kind items crafted by local artists. Shoppers can find traditional Polish pottery, handmade textiles, jewelry, and more. These shops are often located in charming areas, allowing visitors to enjoy the city's atmosphere while browsing.

Notable Shops:

- **Podlaskie Folklore**: This shop showcases locally crafted goods that highlight the region's rich heritage, including embroidered tablecloths, hand-painted ceramics, and folklore-inspired jewelry. The items here make perfect gifts or souvenirs for those looking to bring a piece of Białystok's culture home.

- **Galeria Slendzińskich**: Located within the Slendzinski Gallery, this small shop is filled with art pieces, prints, and crafts inspired by Podlaskie folklore and local artists.

Shopping Tips:

- **Buy Locally**: Look for certified local crafts that support the region's artists. Each purchase helps preserve and celebrate local traditions and techniques.

- **Unique Finds**: Don't miss handcrafted goods like **wycinanki** (Polish paper cutouts) or **bursztyn** (amber jewelry), which are especially popular in the region.

8.3 Souvenirs and Gifts

Białystok has a selection of specialty shops perfect for souvenir hunters. From traditional crafts to unique food items, travelers can find memorable gifts that capture the essence of the region. Local markets and small boutiques often carry distinctive items that are unavailable in larger retail stores, making them ideal for anyone wanting a truly authentic memento.

Recommended Souvenirs:

- **Bison Grass Vodka**: Known as Żubrówka, this vodka is infused with bison grass, giving it a unique flavor. It's a popular Polish specialty and makes a great gift for friends back home.

- **Regional Food Products**: Look for honey from nearby forests, herbal teas, or smoked sausages, all of which capture the natural richness of Podlasie.

- **Podlaskie Embroidery**: Intricate embroidered linens and garments are widely recognized and make beautiful keepsakes or gifts.

8.4 Farmers Markets and Local Produce

Białystok's farmers markets are must-visit destinations for food lovers. These markets showcase the region's freshest produce, including seasonal fruits, vegetables, cheeses, and meats. Shoppers can meet local farmers and producers, learn about Podlasie's agricultural traditions, and taste the flavors of the area.

Popular Markets:

- **Rynek Kościuszki**: This market square hosts seasonal markets where vendors sell everything from fresh produce to handmade crafts. It's an excellent spot to find local food items, including freshly baked bread, honey, and preserves.

- **Bazar Hetmańska**: A bustling open-air market where locals shop for fresh fruits, vegetables, and meats. It's a lively place to experience the local lifestyle and pick up ingredients for a homemade Polish meal.

Tips for Visitors:

- **Cash Payments**: Some stalls may only accept cash, so it's a good idea to carry local currency.

- **Try Before You Buy**: Many vendors offer samples, so you can try fresh cheeses or sausages before making a purchase.

Chapter 9: Białystok for Families and Kids

Chapter Overview: Białystok has many family-friendly attractions, offering activities for all ages. This chapter covers engaging experiences like outdoor parks, educational museums, and family-oriented dining. Whether you're looking for a full day of adventure or a relaxed afternoon with the family, this guide has something for everyone.

9.1 Kid-Friendly Attractions

Białystok offers a range of attractions that cater specifically to kids, blending fun with education. From interactive museums to unique play centers, these destinations allow children to explore, learn, and have a great time.

Top Kid-Friendly Attractions:

- **Akcent Zoo**: This compact zoo in Białystok is a favorite among families. It's home to a variety of animals, including wolves, bison, and deer, all of which are native to the region. The zoo has shaded paths and picnic areas, making it a great spot for a leisurely day out. Kids will enjoy seeing these animals up close while learning about local wildlife.

- **Fikoland Play Center**: Perfect for rainy days, Fikoland is an indoor play area featuring slides, trampolines, climbing walls, and ball pits. It's designed for children of various ages, and parents can relax in the café while their kids enjoy supervised play.

Family Tips:

- **Timing Visits**: Mornings and weekdays are usually less crowded, making these attractions easier to explore.

- **Guided Zoo Walks**: Akcent Zoo sometimes offers guided walks where children can learn about animal care and conservation efforts.

9.2 Outdoor Parks and Playgrounds

Białystok has plenty of outdoor parks and playgrounds where kids can burn off energy while enjoying nature. These parks often feature walking trails, picnic spots, and playgrounds, offering a relaxing environment for family fun.

Recommended Parks:

- **Park Planty**: This lush, expansive park in the heart of Białystok is a go-to for families. It features a large playground, shaded picnic areas, and beautiful flower gardens. The park's walking paths are stroller-friendly, making it easy for families with young children to navigate.

- **Branicki Palace Gardens**: These gardens are a beautiful spot for families, especially those with an interest in history. While kids can explore the open spaces and fountains, parents can enjoy the scenic views of the Baroque-style gardens. It's also a fantastic location for family photos.

Outdoor Fun Tips:

- **Seasonal Activities**: In summer, the parks often host events like outdoor concerts, making the experience even more enjoyable for families.

- **Bring Snacks**: Some parks don't have nearby food vendors, so packing snacks or a picnic is a good idea for a hassle-free outing.

9.3 Family-Friendly Dining

Białystok has a variety of family-friendly restaurants and cafes that cater to younger diners. These spots often feature children's menus, high chairs, and play areas to make dining enjoyable for the whole family.

Top Family Dining Options:

- **Restauracja Kawelin**: Known for its welcoming atmosphere and Polish cuisine, Restauracja Kawelin has a diverse menu that includes both adult and kid-friendly dishes. The restaurant offers a cozy play corner, allowing children to stay entertained while waiting for their meal.

- **Gramoffon Café**: This relaxed café is perfect for breakfast or lunch with children. It offers a dedicated kids' menu, and the staff are known for being accommodating to families. The café also has a small bookshelf with children's books to keep young guests entertained.

Dining Tips:

- **Reserve Ahead**: Family-friendly restaurants can get busy, especially on weekends, so it's a good idea to make a reservation.

- **Local Flavors for Kids**: Encourage kids to try Polish favorites like pierogi (dumplings) with fruit fillings or potato pancakes, as these dishes are often a hit with younger diners.

9.4 Educational Museums and Activities

Białystok has several museums and educational centers with interactive exhibits geared toward children. These venues combine learning with hands-on activities, making them both fun and enriching for young visitors.

Notable Educational Experiences:

- **Museum of the History of Medicine and Pharmacy**: Located at the Medical University of Białystok, this museum offers interactive exhibits and workshops that make learning about medicine's past fun for children. Kids can see old medical equipment and participate in hands-on activities that teach them about the history of healthcare.

- **Podlaskie Museum of Folk Culture**: This open-air museum is a fantastic place for children to learn about traditional Polish village life. With historic wooden cottages, traditional farming tools, and craft demonstrations, it offers a glimpse into Poland's past. Kids can even try activities like weaving or pottery, making for a memorable, immersive experience.

Tips for Parents:

- **Engage with Guides**: Many museums have knowledgeable guides who are great at explaining exhibits in a way that's accessible to kids.

- **Check for Family Workshops**: Some museums offer weekend workshops or special activities tailored for families, which can make the experience even more engaging.

Chapter 10: Practical Information and Traveler Tips

Chapter Overview: This chapter is designed to help travelers navigate Białystok with ease by providing crucial information on safety, health services, money matters, and respectful cultural practices. With these tips, visitors can enjoy a well-prepared and worry-free stay.

10.1 Safety and Emergency Contacts

Białystok is generally a safe city, with low crime rates and a friendly atmosphere. However, it's always wise to be prepared for emergencies. This section will cover local emergency numbers, key contacts, and tips for staying safe.

Key Contacts and Emergency Numbers:

- **Emergency Number (General)**: 112 - This is the EU-wide emergency number for police, ambulance, and fire services.

- **Police**: 997 - Call this number for assistance from the local police.

- **Ambulance**: 999 - In case of a medical emergency, this will connect you with emergency medical services.

- **Fire Department**: 998 - For fire-related emergencies or hazards, contact the fire department.

Safety Tips:

- **Secure Belongings**: Pickpocketing can happen in crowded areas, so keep valuables secured and avoid displaying large amounts of cash.

- **Evening Safety**: While the city is generally safe, it's wise to stay alert when walking in quieter areas late at night.

10.2 Health and Medical Care in Białystok

Access to healthcare in Białystok is good, with several clinics, hospitals, and pharmacies throughout the city. This section will provide guidance on where to seek medical assistance, types of healthcare available, and useful tips for managing health during your stay.

Hospitals and Clinics:

- **University Clinical Hospital in Białystok**: This is one of the largest hospitals in the region and has a good reputation for its healthcare services. It also has an emergency department, which is useful for travelers requiring urgent care.

- **Białystok Medical Center**: This center offers outpatient services, including general practitioners and some specialists.

Healthcare Tips:

- **Travel Insurance**: It's advisable to have comprehensive travel insurance that covers healthcare. EU citizens with a European Health Insurance Card (EHIC) can access medical services at reduced costs.

- **Pharmacies**: Pharmacies, or **apteka**, are found throughout the city, and most staff can assist with basic medical advice. Look for a 24-hour pharmacy in case of emergencies.

10.3 Money Matters and Currency Exchange

Poland's currency is the Polish złoty (PLN), and Białystok has plenty of banks, ATMs, and currency exchange offices to help travelers manage their finances.

Money Tips:

- **Currency Exchange**: Exchange offices, called **kantor**, are available in shopping centers and around popular tourist areas. They typically offer better rates than airports, but it's wise to compare rates to ensure the best deal.

- **ATMs and Banks**: ATMs are widespread in Białystok and generally accept major international cards. However, be cautious about fees, as some banks may charge for international withdrawals.

- **Credit Card Usage**: Credit cards are widely accepted in hotels, restaurants, and shops, though smaller businesses may prefer cash.

Budgeting for Your Trip:

- **Meal Costs**: Dining in Białystok is relatively affordable, with meals at mid-range restaurants costing around 30–50 PLN per person. Traditional dishes, such as **pierogi** or **bigos**, are budget-friendly and offer a true taste of local cuisine.

- **Tipping**: Tipping is generally around 10–15% in restaurants, but it is appreciated and not obligatory.

10.4 Local Etiquette and Cultural Tips

Polish culture is warm and polite, and understanding a few cultural norms can go a long way in showing respect. This section will cover general etiquette, respectful behavior, and a few useful phrases in Polish.

Polish Etiquette:

- **Greetings**: A simple "Dzień dobry" (Good day) goes a long way, and shaking hands is common in formal settings. It's also polite to make eye contact when greeting someone.

- **Table Manners**: When dining with locals, wait until everyone is served before beginning the meal, and remember to say "smacznego" (enjoy your meal) as a courtesy.

- **Gift-Giving**: If you're invited to someone's home, bringing flowers, chocolates, or a small gift is appreciated. However, avoid red or white flowers, as they are traditionally used at funerals.

Useful Phrases in Polish:

- **Hello/Goodbye**: Cześć (hello/goodbye, informal) or Dzień dobry (hello, formal)

- **Thank You**: Dziękuję (jen-koo-yeh)

- **Excuse Me**: Przepraszam (pshe-pra-sham)

- **Yes/No**: Tak (yes) / Nie (no)

10.5 Sustainable Travel Practices

Sustainable travel is becoming more important, and Białystok has initiatives in place to encourage eco-friendly practices. This section will include tips on reducing environmental impact while traveling, such as using public transport, minimizing waste, and supporting local businesses.

Sustainable Travel Tips:

- **Public Transport**: Białystok's public transport network is efficient and includes buses that connect most of the city's major points of interest. Opting for public transportation or walking can reduce your environmental footprint and provide a closer look at daily life in Białystok.

- **Eco-Friendly Accommodation**: Some hotels in Białystok have eco-friendly initiatives, such as using renewable energy or reducing single-use plastics. Consider staying at eco-conscious accommodations where possible.

- **Reduce Plastic Waste**: Many local shops and markets use plastic bags, but you can bring a reusable bag for shopping and avoid disposable items.

Chapter 11: Useful Resources

Chapter Overview: To help travelers get the most out of their trip to Białystok, this chapter compiles essential resources, including useful apps, tourist information centers, and trusted sources for booking tours. These resources make planning easier and ensure visitors don't miss any of the city's unique experiences.

11.1 Maps and City Guide Apps

Smartphones make it easier than ever to navigate a new city, and Białystok offers several helpful apps and maps that make getting around simple and stress-free. This section highlights the most popular and reliable digital tools for visitors.

Recommended Apps:

- **Google Maps**: This app remains one of the best for navigating Białystok's streets, finding public transport options, and checking real-time traffic. It's especially useful for mapping out routes to popular attractions or restaurants.

- **Jakdojade**: A must-have app for navigating public transport in Polish cities, including Białystok. It provides detailed information on bus routes, schedules, and fares, making it easier to use public transit efficiently.

- **Polska Travel**: This official app from the Polish Tourism Organization covers major cities and attractions in Poland. It includes guides, event listings, and other insights that can help you discover unique places in Białystok.

Offline Map Options:

- **Maps.me**: A reliable offline map option, Maps.me lets you download a map of Białystok to navigate without data. It includes markers for major attractions, restaurants, and hotels, making it a great backup for travelers.

11.2 Tourist Information Centers

Tourist information centers are a valuable resource for visitors seeking recommendations, maps, or assistance. These centers are staffed by friendly locals who can provide insights on the best things to see and do around Białystok.

Main Tourist Information Centers:

- **Białystok Tourist Information Center (Biuro Informacji Turystycznej)**: Located near Kościuszki Market Square, this center provides free maps, brochures, and advice. Staff are multilingual and can answer questions about tours, transportation, and cultural events.

- **Podlaskie Voivodeship Tourist Information Center**: Located at the Podlaskie Museum, this center offers more specific insights into the cultural and historical aspects of Białystok and the surrounding region. It's an excellent stop for travelers interested in learning about regional traditions and local attractions.

Tips for Visitors:

- **Ask for Recommendations**: The staff at these centers often know about local events, festivals, and exhibitions that may not be widely advertised.

- **Pick Up Brochures**: Brochures and maps from these centers can offer hidden gems or tips on how to navigate popular sites.

11.3 Recommended Books and Websites

To gain a deeper understanding of Białystok and its culture, history, and attractions, several books and websites provide invaluable information. This section will include a curated list of recommended reading and trusted websites for trip planning.

Recommended Books:

- **"The Białystok Story: A Small Town's Struggle Through War and Peace"** by Joshua D. Zimmerman – This book provides a well-rounded perspective on the history of Białystok, focusing on its role during various conflicts. It's an excellent read for history buffs.

- **"Poland: A Historical Atlas"** by Robert P. Lisowski – An illustrated guide to Polish history, including the Podlasie region, offering maps, timelines, and images to provide context on Białystok's place in Polish history.

- **"Podlasie: A Region in Poland"** – This guidebook focuses on Podlasie, including Białystok, and details everything from natural landscapes to cultural traditions, making it perfect for travelers exploring the region.

Useful Websites:

- **Poland.travel**: The official website of Poland's tourism board provides extensive information on attractions, events, and accommodations across the country, including Białystok.

- **Inyourpocket.com**: A trusted resource for European city guides, In Your Pocket offers detailed information on restaurants, accommodations, and cultural attractions in Białystok.

- **Culture.pl**: Operated by the Adam Mickiewicz Institute, this website is ideal for travelers interested in Poland's art, literature, and cultural scene, including Białystok's contributions.

11.4 Contacts for Guided Tours and Excursions

Guided tours offer an excellent way to explore Białystok with local experts. From historical tours to nature excursions in the Podlasie region, there are numerous options for guided experiences that provide in-depth insights.

Top Tour Providers:

- **Explore Białystok**: This tour company specializes in small group and private tours, offering historical walks through Białystok's Jewish quarter, visits to Branicki Palace, and culinary tours that let travelers taste traditional Podlasie cuisine.

- **Podlasie Adventure**: Ideal for nature lovers, this provider offers excursions to the Białowieża Forest and other natural landmarks in the region, with guides knowledgeable about local wildlife, flora, and conservation efforts.

- **Białystok Free Walking Tour**: This pay-what-you-want tour is great for budget-conscious travelers. It covers the main attractions of Białystok, including Kościuszki Market Square, the Cathedral Basilica, and other iconic spots, with informative guides sharing historical context along the way.

Tips for Booking Tours:

- **Book in Advance**: Some popular tours, especially during peak travel seasons, can fill up quickly, so booking ahead is recommended.

- **Check Language Options**: Most tours are available in English and Polish, but it's wise to confirm language options when booking.

Milton Keynes UK
Ingram Content Group UK Ltd.
UKHW042032031224
452078UK00001B/56